By Michael Ondaatje

Coming through Slaughter
Rat Jelly & Other Poems 1963–78
The Collected Works of Billy the Kid

Rat Jelly
and Other
Poems
1963-78

Rat Jelly and Other Poems 1963-78

MICHAEL ONDAATJE

Marion Boyars · London · Boston

First Published in Great Britain in 1980
By Marion Boyars Publishers Ltd.
18 Brewer Street, London W1R 4AS.

Australian distribution by Thomas C. Lothian
4-12 Tattersalls Lane, Melbourne, Victoria 3000.

Copyright © 1980 by Michael Ondaatje

ISBN 0-7145-2687-8 cased edition
ISBN 0-7145-2688-6 paperback edition

The epigraph for the first section, *The Dainty Monsters*, is a translation of an old Indian poem, quoted in *Classical Sanskrit Love Poetry*, ed. W. S. Merwin and J. Moussaiff Masson, © 1977, reprinted by permission of Columbia University Press. The epigraph for the third section, *Pig Glass*, is from Italo Calvino's *Invisible Cities*, © 1969, reprinted by permission of Farrar, Straus and Giroux, Inc.

Printed and bound in Great Britain by
REDWOOD BURN LIMITED
Trowbridge & Esher

This book is for Kim, Quintin, and Griffin

For Christopher, Janet, and Gillian

And in memory of my parents—Mervyn Ondaatje and Doris Gratiaen

Contents

Pig Glass (1973–78)

The Dainty Monsters

BIRDS FOR JANET—THE HERON

The reach

fingers stretching
backbones

the dull
burst of fur
four feet above water

Reflections make them an hourglass

When heron sits
the hairless ankle
rests on a starved knee

he fingers his food
off the leaf of banana

drinks from a stone container

bathes in blue zebra milk

When he sleeps
the soul is jailed
in tightened claws
torn
if he dies in the night

Heron is the true king

eagles only
muscular henchmen
with mad eyes
bedded in black

We found the path
of a heron's suicide
tracks left empty

walking to the centre of the lake

DRAGON

I have been seeing dragons again.
Last night, hunched on a beaver dam,
one clutched a body like a badly held cocktail;
his tail, keeping the beat of a waltz,
sent a morse of ripples to my canoe.

They are not richly bright
but muted like dawns
or the vague sheen on a fly's wing.
Their old flesh drags in folds
as they drop into grey pools,
strain behind a tree.

Finally the others saw one today, trapped,
tangled in our badminton net.
The minute eyes shuddered deep in the creased face
while his throat, strangely fierce, stretched
to release an extinct burning inside:
pathetic loud whispers as four of us
and the excited spaniel surrounded him.

EARLY MORNING, KINGSTON
TO GANANOQUE

The twenty miles to Gananoque
with tangled dust blue grass
burned, and smelling burned
along the highway
is land too harsh for picnics.
Deep in the fields
behind stiff dirt fern
nature breeds the unnatural.

Escaping cows canter white
then black and white
along the median, forming out of mist.
Crows pick at animal accidents,
with swoops lift meals—
blistered groundhogs, stripped snakes
to arch behind a shield of sun.

Somewhere in those fields
they are shaping new kinds of women.

THE DIVERSE CAUSES

for than all erbys and treys renewyth a man and woman,
and in lyke wyse lovers callyth to their mynde olde
jantylnes and olde servyse, and many kynde dedes that
was forgotyn by necylgence

Three clouds and a tree
reflect themselves on a toaster.
The kitchen window hangs scarred,
shattered by winter hunters.

We are in a cell of civilised magic.
Stravinsky roars at breakfast,
our milk is powdered.

Outside, a May god
moves his paws to alter wind
to scatter shadows of tree and cloud.
The minute birds walk confident
jostling the cold grass.
The world not yet of men.

We clean buckets of their sand
to fetch water in the morning,
reach for winter cobwebs,
sweep up moths who have forgotten to waken.
When the children sleep, angled
behind their bottles, you can hear mice prowl.

I turn a page
careful not to break the rhythms
of your sleeping head on my hip,
watch the moving under your eyelid
that turns like fire,
and we have love and the god outside
until ice starts to limp
in brown hidden waterfalls,
or my daughter burns the lake
by reflecting her red shoes in it.

SIGNATURE

The car carried him
racing the obvious moon
beating in the trees like a white bird.

Difficult to make words sing
around your appendix.
The obvious upsets me,
everyone has scars which crawl
into the mystery of swimming trunks.

I was the first appendix in my family.
My brother who was given the stigma
of a rare blood type
proved to have ulcers instead.

The rain fell like applause as I approached the hospital.

It takes seven seconds she said,
strapped my feet,
entered my arm.
I stretched all senses
on *five*
the room closed on me like an eyelid.

At night the harmonica plays,
a whistler joins in respect.
I am a sweating marble saint
full of demerol and sleeping pills.
A man in the armour of shining plaster

walks to my door, then past.
Imagine the rain
falling like white bees on the sidewalk
imagine Snyder
high on poetry and mountains

Three floors down
my appendix
swims in a jar

O world, I shall be buried all over Ontario

HENRI ROUSSEAU AND FRIENDS

for Bill Muysson

In his clean vegetation
the parrot, judicious,
poses on a branch.
The narrator of the scene,
aware of the perfect fruits,
the white and blue flowers,
the snake with an ear for music;
he presides.

The apes
hold their oranges like skulls,
like chalices.
They are below the parrot
above the oranges—
a jungle serfdom which
with this order
reposes.

They are the ideals of dreams.
Among the exactness,
the symmetrical petals,
the efficiently flying angels,
there is complete liberation.
The parrot is interchangeable;
tomorrow in its place
a waltzing man and tiger,
brash legs of a bird.

Greatness achieved
they loll among textbook flowers

and in this pose hang
scattered like pearls
in just as intense a society.
On Miss Adelaide Milton de Groot's walls,
with Lillie P. Bliss in New York.

And there too
in spangled wrists and elbows
and grand façades of cocktails
are vulgarly beautiful parrots, appalled lions,
the beautiful and the forceful locked in suns,
and the slight, careful stepping birds.

BIOGRAPHY

The dog scatters her body in sleep,
paws, finding no ground, whip at air,
the unseen eyeballs reel deep, within.
And waking—crouches,
tacked to humility all day,
children ride her, stretch,
display the black purple lips,
pull hind legs to dance;
unaware that she
tore bulls apart, loosed
heads of partridges,
dreamt blood.

THE REPUBLIC

This house, exact,
coils with efficiency and style.
A different heaven here,
air even is remade in the basement.

The plants fed daily
stand like footmen by the windows,
flush with decent green
and meet the breeze with polish;
no dancing with the wind here.

Too much reason in its element
passions crack the mask in dreams.
While we sleep
the plants in frenzy heave floors apart,
lust with common daisies,
feel rain,
fling their noble bodies, release a fart.
The clock alone, frigid and superior,
swaggers in the hall.

At dawn gardenias revitalize
and meet the morning with decorum.

IN ANOTHER FASHION

The cat performs,
rippling shoulder
on a strip of fence.
Pneumatic scratching
beats each jaw, shows
earrings of scar
through yellow leaves
and laundry.

We must build new myths
to wind up the world,
provoke new christs
with our beautiful women,
bring

plumed
thin boned birds
to claw carpets
to betray
majesty in a sway

Pale birds
with rings on ugly feet

to drink from clear bowls
to mate with our children

APPLICATION FOR A DRIVING LICENSE

Two birds loved
in a flurry of red feathers
like a burst cottonball,
continuing while I drove over them.

I am a good driver, nothing shocks me.

'LOVELY THE COUNTRY OF PEACOCKS'

My daughter cackling in defiance
voices mystic yells like a snake charmer,
a fulica in the afternoon.

Her buddhist stomach is boasted,
there is an interest in toes.
In rusty actions
she struggles for tender goals:
her mother's hair,
the crumpled paper.
Her retaliations to matches,
muscles, and hairy dogs
are all degreed.
Looking on
we wear sentimentality like a curse.

Her body bears, inside the changing flesh,
rivers of collected suns,
jungles of force, coloured birds
and laziness.

FOUR EYES

Naked I lie here
attempting to separate toes
with no help from hands.
You with scattered nightgown
listen to music, hug a knee.

I pick this moment up
with our common eyes
only choose what you can see

a photograph of you with posing dog
a picture with Chagall's red
a sprawling dress.

This moment I broke to record,
walking round the house
to look for paper.
Returning
I saw you, in your gaze,
still netted the picture, the dog.
The music continuing
you were still being unfurled
shaped by the scene.

I would freeze this moment
and in supreme patience
place pianos
and craggy black horses on a beach
and in immobilised time
attempt to reconstruct.

A HOUSE DIVIDED

This midnight breathing
heaves with no sensible rhythm,
is fashioned by no metronome.
Your body, eager
for the extra yard of bed,
reconnoitres and outflanks;
I bend in peculiar angles.

This nightly battle is fought with subtleties:
you get pregnant, I'm sure,
just for extra ground
—immune from kicks now.

Inside you now's another,
thrashing like a fish,
swinging, fighting
for its inch already.

THE TIME AROUND SCARS

A girl whom I've not spoken to
or shared coffee with for several years
writes of an old scar.
On her wrist it sleeps, smooth and white,
the size of a leech.
I gave it to her
brandishing a new Italian penknife.
Look, I said turning,
and blood spat onto her shirt.

My wife has scars like spread raindrops
on knees and ankles,
she talks of broken greenhouse panes
and yet, apart from imagining red feet,
(a nymph out of Chagall)
I bring little to that scene.
We remember the time around scars,
they freeze irrelevant emotions
and divide us from present friends.
I remember this girl's face,
the widening rise of surprise.

And would she
moving with lover or husband
conceal or flaunt it,
or keep it at her wrist
a mysterious watch.
And this scar I then remember
is medallion of no emotion.

I would meet you now
and I would wish this scar
to have been given with
all the love
that never occurred between us.

FOR JOHN, FALLING

Men stopped in the heel of sun,
hum of engines evaporated;
the machine displayed itself bellied with mud
and balanced—immense.

No one ran to where
his tensed muscles curled unusually,
where jaws collected blood,
the hole in his chest the size of fists,
hands clutched to eyes like a blindness.

Arched there he made
ridiculous requests for air.
And twelve construction workers
what should they do but surround
or examine the path of falling.

And the press in bright shirts,
a doctor, the foreman scuffing a mound,
men removing helmets,
the machine above him
shielding out the sun
while he drowned
in the beautiful dark orgasm of his mouth.

THE GOODNIGHT

With the bleak heron Paris
imagine Philoctetes
the powerful fat thighed man,
the bandaged smelling foot
with rivers of bloodshot veins
scattering like trails into his thighs:
a man who roared on an island for ten years,
whose body grew banal
while he stayed humane
behind the black teeth and withering hair.

Imagine in his hands—black
from the dried blood of animals,
a bow of torn silver
that noised arrows loose like a wild heart;

in front of him—Paris
darting and turning, the perfumed stag,
and beyond him the sun
netted in the hills, throwing back his shape,
until the running spider of shadow
gaped on the bandaged foot of the standing man
who let shafts of eagles into the ribs
that were moving to mountains.

PHILOCTETES ON THE ISLAND

Sun moves broken in the trees
drops like a paw
turns sea to red leopard

I trap sharks and drown them
stuffing gills with sand
cut them with coral till
the blurred grey runs
red designs

And kill to fool myself alive
to leave all pity on the staggering body
in order not to shoot an arrow up
and let it hurl
down through my petalling skull
or neck vein, and lie
heaving round the wood in my lung.
That the end of thinking.
Shoot either eye of bird instead
and run and catch it in your hand.

One day a bird went mad
flew blind along the beach
smashed into a dropping wave
out again and plummeted.
Later knocked along the shore.

To slow an animal
you break its foot with a stone
so two run wounded
reel in the bush, flap
bodies at each other
till free of forest
it gallops broken in the sand,
then use a bow
and pin the tongue back down its throat.

With wind the rain wheels like a circus hoof,
aims at my eyes, rakes up the smell of animals
of stone moss, cleans me.
Branches fall like nightmares in the dark
till sun breaks up
and spreads wound fire at my feet

then they smell me,
the beautiful animals

ELIZABETH

Catch, my Uncle Jack said
and oh I caught this huge apple
red as Mrs Kelly's bum.
It's red as Mrs Kelly's bum, I said
and Daddy roared
and swung me on his stomach with a heave.
Then I hid the apple in my room
till it shrunk like a face
growing eyes and teeth ribs.

Then Daddy took me to the zoo
he knew the man there
they put a snake around my neck
and it crawled down the front of my dress.
I felt its flicking tongue
dripping onto me like a shower.
Daddy laughed and said Smart Snake
and Mrs Kelly with us scowled.

In the pond where they kept the goldfish
Philip and I broke the ice with spades
and tried to spear the fishes;
we killed one and Philip ate it,
then he kissed me
with raw saltless fish in his mouth.

My sister Mary's got bad teeth
and said I was lucky, then she said
I had big teeth, but Philip said I was pretty.
He had big hands that smelled.

I would speak of Tom, soft laughing,
who danced in the mornings round the sundial
teaching me the steps from France, turning
with the rhythm of the sun on the warped branches,
who'd hold my breast and watch it move like a snail
leaving his quick urgent love in my palm.
And I kept his love in my palm till it blistered.

When they axed his shoulders and neck
the blood moved like a branch into the crowd.
And he staggered with his hanging shoulder
cursing their thrilled cry, wheeling,
waltzing in the French style to his knees
holding his head with the ground,
blood settling on his clothes like a blush;
this way
when they aimed the thud into his back.

And I find cool entertainment now
with white young Essex, and my nimble rhymes.

PETER

I

That spring Peter was discovered, freezing
the maze of bones from a dead cow,
skull and hooves glazed
with a skin of ice.
The warmth in his hands
carved hollows of muscle,
his fingers threading veins on its flank.

In the attempt to capture him
he bit, to defend himself,
three throats and a wrist;
that night villagers found the cow
frozen in red, and Peter
eating a meal beside it.

II

They snared him in evening light,
his body a pendulum
between the walls of the yard,
rearing from shrinking flashes of steel
until they, with a new science,
stretched his heels and limbs,
scarred through the back of his knees
leaving his veins unpinned,
and him singing in the evening air.

Till he fainted, and a brown bitch
nosed his pain, stared in interest,
and he froze into consciousness
to drag his feet to the fountain,
to numb wounds.

III

In the first months of his capture
words were growls, meaningless;
disgust in his tone burned everyone.
At meals, in bed, you heard Peter's howl
in the depths of the castle like a bell.
After the first year they cut out his tongue;

difficult
to unpin a fish's mouth
without the eventual jerk
to empty throat of pin and matter.

There followed months of silence,
then the eventual grunting;
he began to speak with the air of his body,
torturing breath into tones; it was despicable,
they had made a dead animal of his throat.

He was little more than a marred stone,
a baited gargoyle, escaped
from the fountain in the courtyard:
his throat swollen like an arm muscle,
his walk stuttered with limp, his knees straight,
his feet arcing like a compass.

IV

They made a hive for him in the court,
Jason throwing him bones from the table,
the daughter Tara tousling in detail
the hair that collapsed like a nest
over his weaving eyes.
She, with bored innocence,
would pet him like a flower,
place vast kisses on his wrists,
thrilled at scowls and obscenities,
delighted at sudden grins
that opened his face like a dawn.

He ate, bouldered at their feet,
vast hands shaping rice,
and he walked with them on grit drives—
his legs dragged like a suitcase behind him.

V

All this while Peter formed violent beauty.
He carved death on chalices,
made spoons of yawning golden fishes;
forks stemmed from the tongues of reptiles,
candle holders bent like the ribs of men.

He made fragments of people: breasts
in the midst of a girl's stride,
a head burrowed in love,
an arm swimming—fingers heaved
to nose barricades of water.

His squat form, the rippled arms
of seaweeded hair,
the fingers black, bent from moulding silver,
poured all his strength
into the bare reflection of eyes

VI

Then Tara grew.

When he first saw her, tall,
ungainly as trees,
her fat knees dangled his shoulders
as her hips rode him,
the court monster, she
swaying from side to side, held
only by the grip of her thighs
on his obtuse neck—
she bending over him,
muttering giggles at his eyes,
covering his creased face with her hair.

And he made golden spiders for her
and silver frogs, with opal glares.

And as she grew, her body
burned its awkwardness.
The full bones roamed
in brown warm skin.
The ridge in her back broadened,
her dress hid seas of thighs,
arms trailed to adjust hair that paused
like a long bird at her shoulder;
and vast brown breasts
restless at each gesture
clung to her body like new sea beasts.

And she smiled cool at Peter now,
a quiet hand received gifts from him,
and her fingers, poised,
touched
to generate expressions.

VII

An arm held her, splayed
its fingers like a cross at her neck
till he could feel fear thrashing at her throat,
while his bent hands tore the sheet of skirt,
lifted her, buttock and neck to the table.
Then laying arm above her breasts
he shaped her body like a mould,
the stub of tongue sharp as a cat, cold,
dry as a cat, rasping neck and breasts
till he poured loathing of fifteen years on her,
a vat of lush oil, staining,
the large soft body like a whale.

Then he lay there breathing at her neck
his face wet from her tears
that glued him to her pain.

Rat Jelly

"*Deep colour and big, shaggy nose. Rather a jumbly, untidy sort of wine, with fruitiness shooting off one way, firmness another, and body pushing about underneath. It will be as comfortable and comforting as the 1961 Nuits St Georges when it has pulled its ends in and settled down.*"

—MAGAZINE DESCRIPTION OF A WINE

BILLBOARDS

"Even his jokes were exceedingly drastic."

My wife's problems with husbands, houses,
her children that I meet
at stations in Kingston, in Toronto, in London Ontario
—they come down the grey steps
bright as actors after their drugged four hour ride
of spilled orange juice and comics
(when will they produce a gun and shoot me
at Union Station by Gate 4?)
Reunions for Easter egg hunts
kite flying, Christmases.
They descend on my shoulders every holiday.
All this, I was about to say,
invades my virgin past.

When she lay beginning
this anthology of kids
I moved—blind but senses
jutting faux pas, terrible humour,
shifted with a sea of persons,
breaking when necessary
into smaller self sufficient bits of mercury.
My mind a carefully empty diary
till I hit the barrier reef
that was my wife—
                    there
the right bright fish
among the coral.

With her came the locusts of history—
innuendoes she had missed
varied attempts at seduction (even rape)
dogs who had been bred
and killed by taxis or brain disease.
Numerous problems I was unequal to.
Here was I trying to live
with a neutrality so great
I'd have nothing to think of,
just to sense
and kill it in the mind.
Nowadays I somehow get the feeling
I'm in a complex situation,
one of several billboard posters
blending in the rain.

I am writing this with a pen my wife has used
to write a letter to her first husband.
On it is the smell of her hair.
She must have placed it down between sentences
and thought, and driven her fingers round her skull
gathered the slightest smell of her head
and brought it back to the pen.

KIM, AT HALF AN INCH

Brain is numbed
is body touch
and smell, warped light

hooked so close
her left eye
is only a golden blur
her ear a vast
musical instrument of flesh

The moon spills off my shoulder
slides into her face

GOLD AND BLACK

At night the gold and black slashed bees come
pluck my head away. Vague thousands drift
leave brain naked stark as liver
each one carries atoms of flesh, they
walk my body in their fingers.
The mind stinks out.

In the black Kim is turning
a geiger counter to this pillow.
She cracks me open like a lightbulb.

Love, the real,
terrifies
the dreamer in his riot cell.

NOTES FOR THE LEGEND OF SALAD WOMAN

Since my wife was born
she must have eaten
the equivalent of two-thirds
of the original garden of Eden.
Not the dripping lush fruit
or the meat in the ribs of animals
but the green salad gardens of that place.
The whole arena of green
would have been eradicated
as if the right filter had been removed
leaving only the skeleton of coarse brightness.

All green ends up eventually
churning in her left cheek.
Her mouth is a laundromat of spinning drowning herbs.
She is never in fields
but is sucking the pith out of grass.
I have noticed the very leaves from flower decorations
grow sparse in their week long performance in our house.
The garden is a dust bowl.

On our last day in Eden as we walked out
she nibbled the leaves at her breasts and crotch.
But there's none to touch
none to equal
the Chlorophyll Kiss

POSTCARD FROM PICCADILLY STREET

Dogs are the unheralded voyeurs of this world.
When we make love
the spaniel shudders
walks out of the room,
she's had her fill of children now

but the bassett—for whom
we've pretty soon got to find a love object
apart from furniture or visitors' legs—
jumps on the bed and watches.

It is a catching habit having a spectator
and appeals to the actor in both of us,
in spite of irate phone calls from the SPCA
who claim we are corrupting minors
(the dog being one and a half).

We have moved to elaborate audiences now.
At midnight we open the curtains
turn out the light
and imagine the tree outside
full of sparrows
with infra red eyes.

THE STRANGE CASE

My dog's assumed my alter ego.
Has taken over—walks the house
phallus hanging wealthy and raw
in front of guests, nuzzling
head up skirts
while I direct my mandarin mood.

Last week driving the baby sitter home.
She, unaware dog sat in the dark back seat,
talked on about the kids' behaviour.
On Huron Street the dog leaned forward
and licked her ear.
The car going 40 miles an hour
she seemed more amazed
at my driving ability
than my indiscretion.

It was only the dog I said.
Oh she said.
Me interpreting her reply all the way home.

DATES

It becomes apparent that I miss great occasions.
My birth was heralded by nothing
but the anniversary of Winston Churchill's marriage.
No monuments bled, no instruments
agreed on a specific weather.
It was a seasonal insignificance.

I console myself with my mother's eighth month.
While she sweated out her pregnancy in Ceylon
a servant ambling over the lawn
with a tray of iced drinks,
a few friends visiting her
to placate her shape, and I
drinking the life lines,
Wallace Stevens sat down in Connecticut
a glass of orange juice at his table
so hot he wore only shorts
and on the back of a letter
began to write 'The Well Dressed Man with a Beard'.

That night while my mother slept
her significant belly cooled
by the bedroom fan
Stevens put words together
that grew to sentences
and shaved them clean and
shaped them, the page suddenly
becoming thought where nothing had been,
his head making his hand
move where he wanted
and he saw his hand was saying
the mind is never finished, no, never
and I in my mother's stomach was growing
as were the flowers outside the Connecticut windows.

WHITE ROOM

dear thin lady
you bend over your stomach
and your body is cool fruit

skin covers stray bones on your back
as sand envelops scattered fragments
of a wrecked aircraft

You are bending over your stomach
I am descending
like helicopters onto the plain

and we collapse
as flesh
within the angles of the room

GRIFFIN OF THE NIGHT

I'm holding my son in my arms
sweating after nightmares
small me
fingers in his mouth
his other fist clenched in my hair
small me
sweating after nightmares

LETTERS & OTHER WORLDS

"for there was no more darkness for him and, no doubt
like Adam before the fall, he could see in the dark"

My father's body was a globe of fear
His body was a town we never knew
He hid that he had been where we were going
His letters were a room he seldom lived in
In them the logic of his love could grow

My father's body was a town of fear
He was the only witness to its fear dance
He hid where he had been that we might lose him
His letters were a room his body scared

He came to death with his mind drowning.
On the last day he enclosed himself
in a room with two bottles of gin, later
fell the length of his body
so that brain blood moved
to new compartments
that never knew the wash of fluid
and he died in minutes of a new equilibrium.

His early life was a terrifying comedy
and my mother divorced him again and again.
He would rush into tunnels magnetized
by the white eye of trains
and once, gaining instant fame,
managed to stop a Perahara in Ceylon
—the whole procession of elephants dancers
local dignitaries—by falling
dead drunk onto the street.

As a semi-official, and semi-white at that,
the act was seen as a crucial
turning point in the Home Rule Movement
and led to Ceylon's independence in 1948.

(My mother had done her share too—
her driving so bad
she was stoned by villagers
whenever her car was recognized)

For 14 years of marriage
each of them claimed he or she
was the injured party.
Once on the Colombo docks
saying goodbye to a recently married couple
my father, jealous
at my mother's articulate emotion,
dove into the waters of the harbour
and swam after the ship waving farewell.
My mother pretending no affiliation
mingled with the crowd back to the hotel.

Once again he made the papers
though this time my mother
with a note to the editor
corrected the report—saying he was drunk
rather than broken hearted at the parting of friends.
The married couple received both editions
of *The Ceylon Times* when their ship reached Aden.

And then in his last years
he was the silent drinker,

the man who once a week
disappeared into his room with bottles
and stayed there until he was drunk
and until he was sober.

There speeches, head dreams, apologies,
the gentle letters, were composed.
With the clarity of architects
he would write of the row of blue flowers
his new wife had planted,
the plans for electricity in the house,
how my half-sister fell near a snake
and it had awakened and not touched her.
Letters in a clear hand of the most complete empathy
his heart widening and widening and widening
to all manner of change in his children and friends
while he himself edged
into the terrible acute hatred
of his own privacy
till he balanced and fell
the length of his body
the blood screaming in
the empty reservoir of bones
the blood searching in his head without metaphor

WE'RE AT THE GRAVEYARD

Stuart Sally Kim and I
watching still stars
or now and then sliding stars
like hawk spit to the trees.
Up there the clear charts,
the systems' intricate branches
which change with hours and solstices,
the bone geometry of moving from there, to there.

And down here—friends
whose minds and bodies
shift like acrobats to each other.
When we leave, they move
to an altitude of silence.

So our minds shape
and lock the transient,
parallel these bats
who organize the air
with thick blinks of travel.
Sally is like grey snow in the grass.
Sally of the beautiful bones
pregnant below stars.

WAR MACHINE

Think I don't like people   NO
like some dont like many
love wife kids dogs couple of friends
hate art which what all talk about
all the time is what they talk about
like monopoly volleyball cards ping pong
tennis late movies hitchcock sergio leone
movie scandal O I can tell you stories
30 jayne mansfield stories that
will give erections all around the room
they'll come at you like non-fiction whips
stories too bout vivien leigh princess margaret
frank sinatra the night he beat up mia farrow

Perhaps
wd like to live mute
all day long
not talk

just listen to the loathing

RAT JELLY

See the rat in the jelly
steaming dirty hair
frozen, bring it out on a glass tray
split the pie four ways and eat
I took great care cooking this treat for you
and tho it looks good to yuh
and tho it smells of the Westinghouse still
and tastes of exotic fish or
maybe the expensive arse of a cow
I want you to know it's rat
steamy dirty hair and still alive

(caught him last sunday
thinking of the fridge, thinking of you.

BREAKING GREEN

Yesterday a Euclid took trees. Bright green
it beat at one till roots tilted
once more, machine in reverse, back ten yards
then forward and tore it off.
The Euclid moved away with it
returned, lifted ground
and levelled the remaining hollow.

And so earth was fresh, dark
a thick smell rising
where the snake lay.
The head grazed ribbon rich
eyes bright as gas.

The Euclid throttled and moved over the snake.
We watched blades dig in skin
and laughed, nothing had happened,
it continued to move bright at our boots.

The machine turned, tilted blade
used it as a spade
jerking onto the snake's back.
It slid away.
        The driver angry then
jumped from the seat and caught the slither
head hooking round to snap his hand
but the snake was being swung already.

It was flying head out fast
as propellers forming green daze
a green gauze through which we saw the man
smile a grimace of pain as his arm tired
snake hurling round and round mouth arched open
till he turned and intercepted
the head with the Euclid blade.

Then he held the neck in his fist
brought his face close
to look at the crashed head
the staring eyes the same
all but the lower teeth
now locked in the skull.

The head was narrower now.
He blocked our looks at it.
The death was his. He
folded the scarless body
and tossed it like a river into the grass.

SULLIVAN AND THE IGUANA

The iguana is a comedian
erasing his body to death,
he is a gladiator retired after performance,
a general waiting for war overseas,
he is as secure about his sex as Tiresias

,thought Sullivan, his feet on the table.
In the room he looks across
to his green friend sleeping over the bulb
who has ignored the clover and vetch
that Sullivan picked in deserted lots.

Sullivan is alone
coiling in the room's light.
From his window he looks down
onto the traffic, people's heads,
he leaves his garbage and soiled grit outside the door.
The room has little furniture.
He pours meals out of tins and packages
and after midnight aims his body to the bed.
From there, every few weeks,
Sullivan watches the ancient friend undress
out of his skin in the rectangle of light
and become young and brilliant green.
Sullivan's brain exercises under the flesh.

Sullivan
,thought the iguana,
can turn the light on can turn it off
can open the cage
can hand in clover or hand in lettuce
can forget to change the water.

LOOP

My last dog poem.
I leave behind all social animals
including my dog who takes
30 seconds dismounting from a chair.
Turn to the one
who appears again on roads
one eye torn out and chasing.

He is only a space filled
and blurred with passing,
transient as shit—will fade
to reappear somewhere else.

He survives the porcupine, cars, poison,
fences with their spasms of electricity.
Vomits up bones, bathes at night
in Holiday Inn swimming pools.

And magic in his act of loss.
The missing eye travels up
in a bird's mouth, and into the sky.
Departing family. It is loss only of flesh
no more than his hot spurt across a tree.

He is the one you see at Drive-Ins
tearing silent into garbage
while societies unfold in his sky.
The bird lopes into the rectangle nest of images

and parts of him move on.

NEAR ELGINBURG

3 a.m. on the floor mattress.
In my pyjamas a moth beats frantic
my heart is breaking loose.

I have been dreaming of a man
who places honey on his forehead before sleep
so insects come tempted by liquid
to sip past it into the brain.
In the morning his head contains wings
and the soft skeletons of wasp.

Our suicide into nature.
That man's seduction
so he can beat the itch
against the floor and give in
move among the sad remnants
of those we have destroyed,
the torn code these animals ride to death on.
Grey fly on windowsill
white fish by the dock
heaved like a slimy bottle into the deep,
to end up as snake
heckled by children and cameras
as he crosses lawns of civilisation.

We lie on the floor mattress
lost moths walk on us
waterhole of flesh, want
this humiliation under the moon.
Till in the morning we are surrounded
by dark virtuous ships
sent by the kingdom of the loon.

HERON REX

Mad kings
blood lines introverted, strained pure
so the brain runs in the wrong direction

they are proud of their heritage of suicides
—not just the ones who went mad
balancing on that goddamn leg, but those

whose eyes turned off
the sun and imagined it
those who looked north, those who
forced their feathers to grow in
those who couldn't find the muscles in their arms
who drilled their beaks into the skin
those who could speak
and lost themselves in the foul connections
who crashed against black bars in a dream of escape
those who moved round the dials of imaginary clocks
those who fell asleep and never woke
who never slept and so dropped dead
those who attacked the casual eyes of children and were led away
and those who faced corners forever
those who exposed themselves and were led away
those who pretended broken limbs, epilepsy,
who managed to electrocute themselves on wire
those who felt their skin was on fire and screamed
                                    and were led away

There are ways of going
physically mad, physically
mad when you perfect the mind

where you sacrifice yourself for the race
when you are the representative when you allow
yourself to be paraded in the cages
celebrity a razor in the body

These small birds so precise
frail as morning neon
they are royalty melted down
they are the glass core at the heart of kings
yet 15 year old boys could enter the cage
and break them in minutes
as easily as a long fingernail

TAKING

It is the formal need
to suck blossoms out of the flesh
in those we admire
planting them private in the brain
and cause fruit in lonely gardens.

To learn to pour the exact arc
of steel still soft and crazy
before it hits the page.
I have stroked the mood and tone
of hundred year dead men and women
Emily Dickinson's large dog, Conrad's beard
and, for myself,
removed them from historical traffic.
Having tasted their brain. Or heard
the wet sound of a death cough.
Their idea of the immaculate moment is now.

The rumours pass on
the rumours pass on
are planted
till they become a spine.

BURNING HILLS

for Kris and Fred

So he came to write again
in the burnt hill region
north of Kingston. A cabin
with mildew spreading down walls.
Bullfrogs on either side of him.

Hanging his lantern of Shell Vapona Strip
on a hook in the centre of the room
he waited a long time. Opened
the Hilroy writing pad, yellow Bic pen.
Every summer he believed would be his last.
This schizophrenic season change, June to September,
when he deviously thought out plots
across the character of his friends.
Sometimes barren as fear going nowhere
or in habit meaningless as tapwater.
One year maybe he would come and sit
for 4 months and not write a word down
would sit and investigate colours, the
insects in the room with him.
What he brought: a typewriter
tins of ginger ale, cigarettes. A copy of *StrangeLove*,
of *The Intervals*, a postcard of Rousseau's *The Dream*.
His friends' words were strict as lightning
unclothing the bark of a tree, a shaved hook.
The postcard was a test pattern by the window
through which he saw growing scenery.
Also a map of a city in 1900.

Eventually the room was a time machine for him.
He closed the rotting door, sat down
thought pieces of history. The first girl
who in a park near his school
put a warm hand into his trousers
unbuttoning and finally catching the spill
across her wrist, he in the maze of her skirt.
She later played the piano
when he had tea with the parents.
He remembered that surprised—
he had forgotten for so long.
Under raincoats in the park on hot days.

The summers were layers of civilisation in his memory
they were old photographs he didn't look at anymore
for girls in them were chubby not as perfect as in his mind
and his ungovernable hair was shaved to the edge of skin.
His friends leaned on bicycles
were 16 and tried to look 21
the cigarettes too big for their faces.
He could read those characters easily
undisguised as wedding pictures.
He could hardly remember their names
though they had talked all day, exchanged styles
and like dogs on a lawn hung around the houses of girls
waiting for night and the devious sex-games with their simple plots.

Sex a game of targets, of throwing firecrackers
at a couple in a field locked in hand-made orgasms,
singing dramatically in someone's ear along with the record

'How do you think I feel / you know our love's not real
The one you're mad about / Is just a gad-about
How do you think I feel'
He saw all that complex tension the way his children would.

There is one picture that fuses the 5 summers.
Eight of them are leaning against a wall
arms around each other
looking into the camera and the sun
trying to smile at the unseen adult photographer
trying against the glare to look 21 and confident.
The summer and friendship will last forever.
Except one who was eating an apple. That was him
oblivious to the significance of the moment.
Now he hungers to have that arm around the next shoulder.
The wretched apple is fresh and white.

Since he began burning hills
the Shell strip has taken effect.
A wasp is crawling on the floor
tumbling over, its motor fanatic.
He has smoked 5 cigarettes.
He has written slowly and carefully
with great love and great coldness.
When he finishes he will go back
hunting for the lies that are obvious.

KING KONG MEETS WALLACE STEVENS

Take two photographs—
Wallace Stevens and King Kong
(Is it significant that I eat bananas as I write this?)

Stevens is portly, benign, a white brush cut
striped tie. Businessman but
for the dark thick hands, the naked brain
the thought in him.

Kong is staggering
lost in New York streets again
a spawn of annoyed cars at his toes.
The mind is nowhere.
Fingers are plastic, electric under the skin.
He's at the call of Metro-Goldwyn-Mayer.

Meanwhile W. S. in his suit
is thinking chaos is thinking fences.
In his head—the seeds of fresh pain
his exorcising,
the bellow of locked blood.

The hands drain from his jacket,
pose in the murderer's shadow.

SPIDER BLUES

"Well I made them laugh, I wish I could make them cry."
—David McFadden*

My wife has a smell that spiders go for.
At night they descend saliva roads
down to her dreaming body.
They are magnetized by her breath's rhythm,
leave their own constructions
for succulent travel across her face and shoulder.
My own devious nightmares
are struck to death by her shrieks.

About the spiders.
Having once tried to play piano
and unable to keep both hands
segregated in their intent
I admire the spider, his control classic,
his eight legs finicky,
making lines out of the juice in his abdomen.
A kind of writer I suppose.
He thinks a path and travels
the emptiness that was there
leaves his bridge behind
looking back saying Jeez
did I do that?
and uses his ending
to swivel to new regions
where the raw of feelings exist.

Spiders like poets are obsessed with power.
They write their murderous art which sleeps
like stars in the corner of rooms,
a mouth to catch audiences
weak   broken   sick

And spider comes to fly, says
Love me I can kill you, love me

my intelligence has run rings about you
love me, I kill you for the clarity that
comes when roads I make are being made
love me, antisocial, lovely.
And fly says, O no
no your analogies are slipping
no I choose who I die with
you spider poets are all the same
you in your close vanity of making,
you minor drag, your saliva stars always
soaking up the liquid from our atmosphere.
And the spider in his loathing
crucifies his victims in his spit
making them the art he cannot be.

So. The ending we must arrive at.
                              ok folks.
Nightmare for my wife and me:

It was a large white room
and the spiders had thrown
their scaffolds off the floor
onto four walls and the ceiling.
They had surpassed themselves this time
and with the white roads
their eight legs built with speed
they carried her up—her whole body
into the dreaming air so gently
she did not wake or scream.
What a scene. So many trails
the room was a shattered pane of glass.
Everybody clapped, all the flies.
They came and gasped,
everybody cried at the beauty
ALL
except the working black architects
and the lady locked in their dream   their theme

'THE GATE IN HIS HEAD'

for Victor Coleman

Victor, the shy mind
revealing the faint scars
coloured strata of the brain,
not clarity but the sense of shift

a few lines, the tracks of thought

Landscape of busted trees
the melted tires in the sun
Stan's fishbowl
with a book inside
turning its pages
like some sea animal
camouflaging itself
the typeface clarity
going slow blonde in the sun full water

My mind is pouring chaos
in nets onto the page.
A blind lover, dont know
what I love till I write it out.
And then from Gibson's your letter
with a blurred photograph of a gull.
Caught vision. The stunning white bird
an unclear stir.

And that is all this writing should be then.
The beautiful formed things caught at the wrong moment
so they are shapeless, awkward
moving to the clear.

CHARLES DARWIN PAYS A VISIT, DECEMBER 1971

View of the coast of Brazil.
A man stood up to shout
at the image of a sailing ship
which was a vast white bird from over the sea
and now ripping its claws into the ocean.
Faded hills of March
painted during the cold morning.
On board ship Charles Darwin sketched clouds.

One of these days the Prime Mover will
paint the Prime Mover out of his sky.
I want a . . . centuries being displaced
. . . faith.

> 23rd of June, 1832.
> He caught sixty-eight species
> of a particularly minute beetle.

The blue thick leaves who greeted him
animals unconscious of celebration
moved slowly into law.
Adam with a watch.
Look past and future, (*I want a . . .*),
ease our way out of the structures
this smell of the cogs
and diamonds we live in.

I am waiting for a new ship, so new
we will think the lush machine
an animal of God.
Weary from travelling over the air and the water
it will sink to its feet at our door.

THE VAULT

Having to put forward candidates for God
I nominate Henri Rousseau and Dr Bucke,
tired of the lizard paradise
whose image banks renew off the flesh of others
—those stories that hate, which are remnants and insults.
Refresh where plants breed to the edge of dream.

I have woken to find myself covered in white sheets
walls and doors, food.
There was no food in the world I left
where I ate the rich air. The bodies of small birds
who died while flying fell into my mouth.
Fruit dripped through our thirst to the earth.

All night the traffic of apes floats across the sky
a worm walks through the gaze of a lion
some birds live all their evenings on one branch.

They are held by the celebration of God's wife.
In Rousseau's *The Dream* she is the naked lady
who has been animal and tree
her breast a suckled orange.
The fibres and fluids of their moral nature
have seeped within her frame.

The hand is outstretched
her fingers move out in
mutual transfusion to the place.
Our low speaking last night
was barely audible among the grunt
of mongrel meditation.

She looks to the left
for that is the direction we leave in
when we fall from her room of flowers.

WHITE DWARFS

This is for people who disappear
for those who descend into the code
and make their room a fridge for Superman
—who exhaust costume and bones that could perform flight,
who shave their moral so raw
they can tear themselves through the eye of a needle
this is for those people
that hover and hover
and die in the ether peripheries

There is my fear
of no words   of
falling without words
over and over   of
mouthing the silence
Why do I love most
among my heroes those
who sail to that perfect edge
where there is no social fuel
Release of sandbags
to understand their altitude—

        that silence of the third cross
        3rd man hung so high and lonely
        we don't hear him say
        say his pain, say his unbrotherhood
        What has he to do with the smell of ladies
        can they eat off his skeleton of pain?

The Gurkhas in Malaya
cut the tongues of mules
so they were silent beasts of burden
in enemy territories
after such cruelty what could they speak of anyway
And Dashiell Hammett in success
suffered conversation and moved
to the perfect white between the words

This white that can grow
is fridge, bed,
is an egg—most beautiful
when unbroken, where
what we cannot see is growing
in all the colours we cannot see

there are those burned out stars
who implode into silence
after parading in the sky
after such choreography what would they wish to speak of   anyway

Pig Glass

"Newly arrived and totally ignorant of the Levantine
languages, Marco Polo could express himself only with
gestures, leaps, cries of wonder and of horror, animal
barkings or hootings, or with objects he took from his
knapsacks—ostrich plumes, pea-shooters, quartzes which
he arranged in front of him . . ."

—ITALO CALVINO

THE AGATHA CHRISTIE BOOKS
BY THE WINDOW

In the long open Vancouver Island room
sitting by the indoor avocados
where indoor spring light
falls on the half covered bulbs

and down the long room light falling
onto the dwarf orange tree
vines from south america
the agatha christie books by the window

Nameless morning
solution of grain and colour

There is this amazing light,
colourless, which falls on the warm
stretching brain of the bulb
that is dreaming avocado

COUNTRY NIGHT

The bathroom light burns over the mirror

In the blackness of the house
beds groan from the day's exhaustion
hold the tired shoulders bruised
and cut legs the unexpected
3 a.m. erections. Someone's dream
involves a saw someone's
dream involves a woman.
We have all dreamed of finding the lost dog.

The last light on upstairs
throws a circular pattern
through the decorated iron vent
to become a living room's moon.

The sofa calls the dog, the cat
in perfect blackness walks over the stove.
In the room of permanent light
cockroaches march on enamel.
The spider with jewel coloured thighs the brown moth
with corporal stripes
                        ascend pipes
and look into mirrors.

All night the truth happens.

MOON LINES, AFTER JIMÉNEZ

Are you going around naked
in the house?

        speaking to moon

from the precise
place of darkness
speaking to
the unnamed woman

The moon has no shoes
undresses itself of cloud
river reflection

In dark bound rooms
the lost men imagine
paths of biography
on their palms

The greatest shipwrecks
are silent
semaphore their bones
through tide
they grow coloured history
wait
for the clock of moon

The abandoned woman
dives through darkness
and then
balances
with the magic fluid of her ear

It is here
it is now
when my thumb
swallows the candlelight

BUYING THE DOG

He's shy Buck McLeish says
stops spray painting the John Deere
stepping out the dark oil smell barn
through a brief patch of Lindsay Ontario sun
and into the mellow light of the kennels

where the dog who has been
in a religious fit of silence
since birth   stands
petrified in his corner.
The other dogs wave their bodies against the fence.
Buck gives us the character of each hound—
he's mental   he's savage
and this one
the one he's going to sell us
is shy.

In the car through all the small towns
Omemee   Fowler's Corners   Jermyn
the dog buries his head in the backseat
for 115 miles the wide eyes
stare into car leather.
Towns the history of his bones
Preneven   Marmora   Actinolite   Enterprise

Bellrock and home.

                    Carefully
the dog puts his feet
like thin white sticks out of the car and
takes off JESUS
like a dolphin
over the fields for all we know
he won't be coming back—

MOVING FRED'S OUTHOUSE /
GERIATRICS OF PINE

All afternoon (while the empty drive-in
screen in the distance promises)
we are moving the two-seater
100 yards across his garden

We turn it over on its top
and over, and as it slowly
falls on its side
the children cheer

60 years old and a change in career
—from these pale yellow flowers emerging
out of the damp wood in the roof
to a room thorough with flight, noise,
and pregnant with the morning's eggs
—a perch for chickens.

Two of us. The sweat.
Our hands under the bottom
then the top as it goes
over, through twin holes the
flowers, running to move the roller, shove,
and everybody screaming to keep the dog away.
Fred the pragmatist—dragging the ancient comic
out of retirement and into a television series
among the charging democracy of rhode island reds

Head over heels across the back lawn
old wood collapsing in our hands

All afternoon the silent space is turned

BUCK LAKE STORE AUCTION

Scrub lawn.

       A chained
dog tense and smelling.
The outhouse.
50 cents for a mattress. 50 cents
for doors that allowed privacy.
What else can you sell?

          A rain
swollen copy of Jack London
a magazine drawing of a rabbit
bordered with finishing nails.
6 chickens, bird cage (empty),
sauerkraut cutting board

down to the rock
          trees

not bothering to look
into the old woman's eyes
as we go in, get a number
have the power to bid
on everything that is exposed.
After an hour in this sun
I expected her to unscrew
her left arm and donate it
to the auctioneer's excitement.

In certain rituals we desire
only what we cannot have.
While for her, Mrs Germain,
this is the needle's eye
where maniacs of heaven select.
Look, I wanted to say,
$10 for the dog
with faded denim eyes

FARRE OFF

There are the poems of Campion I never saw till now
and Wyatt who loved with the best
and suddenly I want 16th century women
round me devious politic aware
of step ladders to the king

Tonight I am alone with dogs and lightning
aroused by Wyatt's talk of women who step
naked into his bedchamber

Moonlight and barnlight constant
lightning every second minute
I have on my thin blue parka
and walk behind the asses of the dogs
who slide under the gate
and sense cattle
deep in the fields

I look out into the dark pasture
past where even the moonlight stops

my eyes are against the ink of Campion

WALKING TO BELLROCK

Two figures in deep water.

Their frames truncated at the stomach
glide along the surface. Depot Creek.
One hundred years ago lumber being driven down this river
tore and shovelled and widened the banks into Bellrock
down past bridges to the mill.

The two figures are walking
as if half sunk in a grey road
their feet tentative, stumbling on stone bottom.
Landscapes underwater. What do the feet miss?
Turtle, watersnake, clam. What do the feet ignore
and the brain not look at, as two figures slide
past George Grant's green immaculate fie!ds
past the splashed blood of cardinal flower on the bank.

Rivers are a place for philosophy but all thought
is about the mechanics of this river is about
stones that twist your ankles
the hidden rocks you walk your knee into—
feet in slow motion and brain and balanced arms
imagining the blind path of foot, underwater sun
suddenly catching the almond coloured legs
the torn old Adidas tennis shoes we wear
to walk the river into Bellrock.

What is the conversation about for three hours
on this winding twisted evasive river to town?
What was the conversation about all summer.

Stan and I laughing joking going summer crazy
as we lived against each other.
To keep warm we submerge. Sometimes
just our heads decapitated
glide on the dark glass.

There is no metaphor here.
We are aware of the heat of the water, coldness of the rain,
smell of mud in certain sections that farts
when you step on it, mud never walked on
so you can't breathe, my god you can't breathe this air
and you swim fast your feet off the silt of history
that was there when the logs went
leaping down for the Rathburn Timber Company 1840–1895
when those who stole logs had to leap
right out of the country if caught.

But there is no history or philosophy or metaphor with us.
The problem is the toughness of the Adidas shoe
its three stripes gleaming like fish decoration.
The story is Russell's arm waving out of the green of a field.

The plot of the afternoon is to get to Bellrock
through rapids, falls, stink water
and reach the island where beer and a towel wait for us.
That night there is not even pain in our newly used muscles
not even the puckering of flesh
and little to tell except you won't
believe how that river winds and when you
don't see the feet you concentrate on the feet.
And all the next day trying to think
what we didn't talk about.
Where was the criminal conversation
broken sentences lost in the splash in wind.

Stan, my crazy summer friend,
why are we both going crazy?
Going down to Bellrock
recognizing home by the colour of barns
which tell us north, south, west,
and otherwise lost in miles and miles of rain
in the middle of this century
following the easy fucking stupid plot to town.

PIG GLASS

Bonjour.   This is pig glass
a piece of cloudy sea

nosed out of the earth by swine
and smoothed into pebble
run it across your cheek
it will not cut you

and this is my hand   a language
which was buried for years   touch it
against your stomach

                        The pig glass
I thought
was the buried eye of Portland Township
slow faded history
waiting to be grunted up
There is no past until you breathe
on such green glass
                        rub it
over your stomach and cheek

The Meeks family used this section
years ago to bury tin
crockery forks dog tags
and each morning
pigs ease up that ocean
redeeming it again
into the possibilities of rust
one morning I found a whole axle
another day a hand crank

but this is pig glass
tested with narrow teeth
and let lie. The morning's green present.
Portland Township jewelry.

There is the band from the ankle of a pigeon
a weathered bill from the Bellrock Cheese Factory
letters in 1925 to a dead mother I
disturbed in the room above the tractor shed.
Journals of family love
servitude to farm weather
a work glove in a cardboard box
creased flat and hard like a flower.

A bottle thrown
by loggers out of a wagon
past midnight
explodes against rock.
This green fragment has behind it
the *booomm* when glass
tears free of its smoothness

now once more smooth as knuckle
a tooth on my tongue.
Comfort that bites through skin
hides in the dark afternoon of my pocket.
Snake shade.
Determined histories of glass.

THE HOUR OF COWDUST

It is the hour we move small
in the last possibilities of light

now the sky opens its blue vault

I thought this hour belonged to my children
bringing cows home
bored by duty swinging a stick,
but this focus of dusk out of dust
is everywhere—here by the Nile
the boats wheeling
like massive half-drowned birds
and I gaze at water that dreams
dust off my tongue,
in this country your mouth
feels the way your shoes look

Everything is reducing itself to shape

Lack of light cools your shirt
men step from barbershops
their skin alive to the air.
All day
dust covered granite hills
and now
suddenly the Nile is flesh
an arm on a bed

In Indian miniatures
I cannot quite remember
what this hour means
—people were small,
animals represented

simply by dust
they stamped into the air.
All I recall of commentaries
are abrupt lovely sentences where
the colour of a bowl
a left foot stepping on a lotus
symbolised separation.
Or stories of gods
creating such beautiful women
they themselves burned in passion
and were reduced to ash.
Women confided to pet parrots
solitary men dreamed into the conch.
So many
graciously humiliated
by the distance of rivers

The boat turns languid
under the hunched passenger
sails
ready for the moon
fill like a lung

there is no longer
depth of perception
it is now possible
for the outline of two boats
to collide silently

THE PALACE

7 a.m.   The hour of red daylight

I walk through palace grounds
waking the sentries
                    scarves
around their neck and mouths
leak breath mist
The gibbons stroll
twenty feet high
through turret arches
and on the edge
of brown parapet
I am alone
            leaning
            into flying air

Ancient howls of a king
who released his aviary
like a wave to the city below
celebrating the day of his birth
and they when fed
would return to his hand
like the payment of grain

All over Rajasthan
palaces die young
                    at this height
                    a red wind
my shirt and sweater cold

From the white city below
a beautiful wail
of a woman's voice rises
300 street transistors
simultaneously playing
the one radio station of Udaipur

USWETAKEIYAWA

Uswetakeiyawa.   The night mile

through the village of tall
thorn leaf fences
sudden odours
which pour through windows of the jeep.

We see nothing, just
the grey silver of the Dutch canal
where bright coloured boats
lap like masks in the night
their alphabets lost in the dark.

No sight but the imagination's
story behind each smell
or now and then a white sarong
pumping its legs on a bicycle
like a moth in the headlights

        and the dogs
who lean out of night
strolling the road
with eyes of sapphire
and hideous body
             so mongrelled
they seem to have woken
to find themselves tricked
into outrageous transformations,
one with the spine of a snake
one with a creature in its mouth

(car lights rouse them
from the purity of darkness)
one that could be a pig
slaughtered lolling
on the carrier of a bike.

This is the dream journey
we travel most nights
returning from Colombo.
A landscape nightmare
unphotographed country.
The road hugs the canal
the canal every mile
puts an arm into the sea.

In daylight women bathe
waist deep beside the road
utterly still as I drive past
their diya reddha cloth
tied under their arms.
Brief sentences of women
lean men with soapy buttocks
their arms stretching up
to pour water over themselves,
or the ancient man in spectacles
crossing the canal
only his head visible
pulling something we cannot see
in the water behind him.
The women surface
bodies the colour of shadow
wet bright cloth
the skin of a mermaid.

In the silence of the night drive
you hear ocean you swallow odours
which change each minute—dried fish
swamp   toddy   a variety of curries
and something we have never been able to recognize.
There is just this thick air
and the aura of dogs
in trickster skin.

Once in the night we saw
something slip into the canal.
There was then the odour we did not recognize.
The smell of a dog losing its shape.

THE WARS

Dusk in Colombo

the Bo tree   dark all day
gathers the last of our light

and in its green rooms which yawn
over Pettah stores
is its own shadow
—hundreds of unseen bats
tuning up the auditorium
in archaic Tamil

Trincomalee
               they whisper
is my brother
source of my exile
long slow miles to the scrub north
whose blossoms are dirty birds
so bright they are extracts of the sea

Swim
      into the north's blue eye
over the milk floor of ocean
that darkens only with depth

The Ray
flies in silence
muttering bubbles to himself

Tread over his avenue

The ancient warrior
whose brother
stole his operatic tongue

                    plunges

in pure muscle
towards his neighbours
bloodless   full
of noon moonlight

only his twin
knows how to charm
the waters against him

SWEET LIKE A CROW

for Hetti Corea, 8 years old

*"The Sinhalese are beyond a doubt one of the least musical
people in the world. It would be quite impossible to have
less sense of pitch, line, or rhythm"*

—PAUL BOWLES

Your voice sounds like a scorpion being pushed
through a glass tube
like someone has just trod on a peacock
like wind howling in a coconut
like a rusty bible, like someone pulling barbed wire
across a stone courtyard, like a pig drowning,
a vattacka being fried
a bone shaking hands
a frog singing at Carnegie Hall.
Like a crow swimming in milk,
like a nose being hit by a mango
like the crowd at the Royal-Thomian match,
a womb full of twins, a pariah dog
with a magpie in its mouth
like the midnight jet from Casablanca
like Air Pakistan curry,
a typewriter on fire, like a spirit in the gas
which cooks your dinner, like a hundred
pappadans being crunched, like someone
uselessly trying to light 3 *Roses* matches in a dark room,
the clicking sound of a reef when you put your head into the sea,
a dolphin reciting epic poetry to a sleepy audience,
the sound of a fan when someone throws brinjals at it,
like pineapples being sliced in the Pettah market
like betel juice hitting a butterfly in mid-air

like a whole village running naked onto the street
and tearing their sarongs, like an angry family
pushing a jeep out of the mud, like dirt on the needle,
like 8 sharks being carried on the back of a bicycle
like 3 old ladies locked in the lavatory
like the sound I heard when having an afternoon sleep
and someone walked through my room in ankle bracelets.

LATE MOVIES WITH SKYLER

All week since he's been home
he has watched late movies alone
terrible one star films and then staggering
through the dark house to his bed
waking at noon to work on the broken car
he has come home to fix.

21 years old and restless
back from logging on Vancouver Island
with men who get rid of crabs with Raid
    2 minutes bending over in agony
    and then into the showers!

Last night I joined him for *The Prisoner of Zenda*
a film I saw three times in my youth
and which no doubt influenced me morally.
Hot coffee bananas and cheese
we are ready at 11.30 for adventure.

At each commercial Sky
breaks into midnight guitar practice
head down playing loud and intensely
till the movie comes on and the music suddenly stops.
Skyler's favourite hours when he's usually alone
cooking huge meals of anything in the frying pan
thumbing through *Advanced Guitar* like a bible.
We talk during the film
and break into privacy during commercials
or get more coffee or push
the screen door open and urinate under the trees.

Laughing at the dilemmas of 1920 heroes
suggestive lines, cutaways to court officials
who raise their eyebrows at least 4 inches
when the lovers kiss . . .
only the anarchy of the evil Rupert of Hentzau
is appreciated.
         And still somehow
by 1.30 we are moved
as Stewart Granger girl-less and countryless
rides into the sunset with his morals and his horse.
The perfect world is over. Banana peels
orange peels ashtrays guitar books.
2 a.m. We stagger through
into the slow black rooms of the house.

I lie in bed fully awake. The darkness
breathes to the pace of a dog's snoring.
The film is replayed to sounds
of an intricate blues guitar.
Skyler is Rupert then the hero.
He will leave in a couple of days
for Montreal or the Maritimes.
In the movies of my childhood the heroes
after skilled swordplay and moral victories
leave with absolutely nothing
to do for the rest of their lives.

SALLIE CHISUM / LAST WORDS
ON BILLY THE KID. 4 A.M.

for Nancy Beatty

The moon hard and yellow where Billy's head is.
I have been moving in my room
these last 5 minutes. Looking for a cigarette.
That is a sin he taught me.
Showed me how to hold it and how to want it.

I had been looking and stepped forward
to feel along the windowsill
and there was the tanned moon head.
His body the shadow of the only tree on the property.

*

I am at the table.
Billy's mouth is trying
to remove a splinter out of my foot.
Tough skin on the bottom of me.
Still. I can feel his teeth
bite precise. And then moving his face back
holding something in his grin, says he's got it.

*

Where have you been I ask
Where have you been he replies

I have been into every room about 300 times
since you were here
I have walked about 60 miles in this house
Where have you been I ask

*

Billy was a fool
he was like those reversible mirrors
you can pivot round and see yourself again

but there is something showing on the other side always.
Sunlight. The shade beside the cupboard

*

He fired two bullets into the dummy
on which I built dresses
where the nipples should have been.
That wasnt too funny, but we laughed a lot.

*

One morning he was still sleeping
I pushed the door and watched him from the hall
he looked like he was having a serious dream.
Concentrating. Angry. As if wallpaper
had been ripped off a wall.

*

Billy's mouth at my foot
removing the splinter.
Did I say that?

*

It was just before lunch one day.

*

I have been alive
37 years since I knew him. He was a fool.
He was like those mirrors I told you about.

*

I am leaning against the bed rail
I have finished my cigarette
now I cannot find the ashtray.
I put it out, squash it
against the window
where the moon is.
In his stupid eyes.

PURE MEMORY / CHRIS DEWDNEY

> *"Listen, it was so savage and brutal and powerful*
> *that even though it happened out of the blue I*
> *knew there was nothing arbitrary about it"*
> —CHRISTOPHER DEWDNEY

1

On a B.C. radio show the man asked me, coffee half way
up to his mouth, what are the books you've liked recently?
Christopher Dewdney's A *Palaeozoic Geology of London
Ontario*. Only I didn't say that, I started stumbling on the
word Palaeozoic . . . Paleo . . . Polio . . . and then it
happened on Geology too until it seemed a disease. I
sounded like an idiot. Meanwhile I was watching the
man's silent gulps. The professional silent gulping of
coffee an inch or two away from the microphone.
Unconcerned with my sinking "live" all over the province.

2

I can't remember where I first met him. Somewhere I
became aware of this giggle. Tan hair, tan face, tan shirt
and a giggle-snort as his head staggered back. His arms
somewhere.

3

The baby. He shows me the revolving globe in the 4
month old kid's crib. Only it has been unscrewed and the
globe turned upside down and rescrewed in that way so
Africa and Asia all swivel upside down. This way he says
she'll have to come to terms with the shapes all over again
when she grows up.

4

He comes to dinner, steps out of the car and transforms
the 10 year old suburban garden into ancient history. Is on
his knees pointing out the age and race and character of
rocks and earth. He loves the Norfolk Pine. I give him a
piece of wood 120 million years old from the tar sands and
he smokes a bit of it. Recently he claims the rest of the
piece is going white.

5

When he was a kid and his parents had guests and he was
eventually told to get to bed he liked to embarrass them by
running under a table and screaming out Don't hit me
Don't hit me.

6

His most embarrassing moment. A poetry reading in
Toronto. He was sitting in the front row and he realised
that he hated the poetry. He looked around discreetly for
the exit but it was a long way away. Then to the right,
quite near him, he saw another door. As a poem ended he
got up and officially walked to the door quickly opened it
went out and closed it behind him. He found himself in a
dark cupboard about 2 feet by 3 feet. It contained nothing.
He waited there a while, then he started to laugh and
giggle. He giggled for 5 minutes and he thinks the
audience could probably hear him. When he had
collected himself he opened the door, came out, walked to
his seat and sat down again.

7

Coach House Press, December 1974. I haven't seen him
for a long time. His face is tough. Something has left his
face. It is not that he is thinner but the face has lost
something distinct and it seems like flesh. But he is not
thinner. He is busy working on his new book *Fovea
Centralis* and I watch him as he sits in the empty back
room upstairs all alone with a computer typesetting
terminal. Has taught himself to use it and tries to teach me
but I don't understand a word and nod and ask how he is.
I can't get over his face. It is "tight", as if a stocking were
over it and he about to perform a robbery. He plucks at the
keys and talks down into the machine. I am relieved when
he starts giggling at something. I tell him I'm coming
down to London in a week and he says he will show me
his butterflies, he has bought two mounted butterflies for a
very good price. If I don't tell anyone he will let me know
where I could get one. A Chinaman in London Ontario
sells them. I start to laugh. He doesn't. This is serious
information, important rare information like the history of
rocks—these frail wings of almost powder have their
genealogies too.

8

His favourite movie is *Earthquake*. He stands in the
middle of his apartment very excited telling me all the
details. He shows me his beautiful fossils, the white that is
on the 120 million year old wood, a small poster of James
Dean hitting his brother in *East of Eden*, and the two very
impressive mounted butterflies.

9

On the bus going back to Toronto I have a drawing of him
by Bob Fones. Wrapped in brown paper it lies above me
on the luggage rack. When the bus swerves I put my arm
out into the dark aisle ready to catch him if it falls. A
strange drawing of him in his cane chair with a plant to
the side of him, reading Frank O'Hara with very oriental
eyes. It was done in 1973, before the flesh left his face.

10

His wife's brain haemorrhage. I could not cope with that.
He is 23 years old. He does. Africa Asia Australia upside
down. Earthquake.

BEARHUG

Griffin calls to come and kiss him goodnight
I yell ok. Finish something I'm doing,
then something else, walk slowly round
the corner to my son's room.
He is standing arms outstretched
waiting for a bearhug. Grinning.

Why do I give my emotion an animal's name,
give it that dark squeeze of death?
This is the hug which collects
all his small bones and his warm neck against me.
The thin tough body under the pyjamas
locks to me like a magnet of blood.

How long was he standing there
like that, before I came?

LIGHT

for Doris Gratiaen

Midnight storm. Trees walking off across the fields in fury
naked in the spark of lightning.
I sit on the white porch on the brown hanging cane chair
coffee in my hand midnight storm midsummer night.
The past, friends and family, drift into the rain shower.
Those relatives in my favourite slides
re-shot from old minute photographs so they now stand
complex ambiguous grainy on my wall.

This is my Uncle who turned up to his marriage
on an elephant. He was a chaplain.
This shy looking man in the light jacket and tie was infamous,
when he went drinking he took the long blonde beautiful hair
of his wife and put one end in the cupboard and locked it
leaving her tethered in an armchair.
He was terrified of her possible adultery
and this way died peaceful happy to the end.
My Grandmother, who went to a dance in a muslin dress
with fireflies captured and embedded in the cloth, shining
and witty. This calm beautiful face
organised wild acts in the tropics.
She hid the mailman in her house
after he had committed murder and at the trial
was thrown out of the court for making jokes at the judge.
Her son became a Q.C.
This is my brother at 6. With his cousin and his sister
and Pam de Voss who fell on a pen-knife and lost her eye.
My Aunt Christie. She knew Harold MacMillan was a spy
communicating with her through pictures in the newspapers.
Every picture she believed asked her to forgive him,
his hound eyes pleading.

Her husband Uncle Fitzroy a doctor in Ceylon had a memory
sharp as scalpels into his 80's
though I never bothered to ask him about anything
—interested then more in the latest recordings of Bobby Darin.

And this is my Mother with her brother Noel in fancy dress.
They are 7 and 8 years old, a hand-coloured photograph,
it is the earliest picture I have. The one I love most.
A picture of my kids at Halloween
has the same contact and laughter.
My Uncle dying at 68, and my Mother a year later dying at 68.
She told me about his death and the day he died
his eyes clearing out of illness as if seeing
right through the room the hospital and she said
he saw something so clear and good his whole body
for a moment became youthful and she remembered
when she sewed badges on his trackshirts.
Her voice joyous in telling me this, her face light and clear.
(My firefly Grandmother also dying at 68).

These are the fragments I have of them, tonight
in this storm, the dogs restless on the porch.
They were all laughing, crazy, and vivid in their prime.
At a party my drunk Father
tried to explain a complex operation on chickens
and managed to kill them all in the process, the guests
having dinner an hour later while my Father slept
and the kids watched the servants clean up the litter
of beaks and feathers on the lawn.

These are their fragments, all I remember,
wanting more knowledge of them. In the mirror and in my kids
I see them in my flesh. Wherever we are
they parade in my brain and the expanding stories
connect to the grey grainy pictures on the wall,
as they hold their drinks or 20 years later
hold grandchildren, pose with favourite dogs,
coming through the light, the electricity, which the storm
destroyed an hour ago, a tree going down by the highway
so that now inside the kids play dominoes by candlelight
and out here the thick rain static the spark of my match

                                                to a cigarette

and the trees across the fields leaving me, distinct
lonely in their own knife scars and cow-chewed bark
frozen in the jagged light as if snapped in their run
the branch arms waving to what was a second ago the dark sky
when in truth like me they haven't moved.
Haven't moved an inch from me.

Acknowledgments

I would like to thank Coach House Press who published *The Dainty Monsters* in 1967 and *Rat Jelly* in 1973.

Also the following magazines and journals which published individual poems: *Canadian Forum, Fiddlehead, Quarry, Alphabet, Open Letter, Duel, Writing, The Tamarack Review, artscanada, IS, White Pelican, Tuatara, Blew Ointment, South Shore, Unicorn Portfolio, Saturday Night, Canadian Literature, Queen's Quarterly, and The Capilano Review*.

My thanks to the Canada Council for their support at various times.

ABOUT THE AUTHOR

MICHAEL ONDAATJE was born in Ceylon/Sri Lanka, where his family had lived for several generations. He left Ceylon at the age of 11 to go to school in England. He came to Canada in 1962.

He lives with his family for part of the year in Toronto (where he teaches at Glendon College, York University), and the rest of the time on a farm north of Kingston, Ontario.

His books include *The Dainty Monsters* (1967), *The Man with 7 Toes* (1969), and *Rat Jelly* (1973). In 1970 his book of poetry and prose called *The Collected Works of Billy the Kid* was published and won the Governor-General's Award. *Coming through Slaughter,* his fictional work on the life and music of the jazzman Buddy Bolden, was published in 1976 and won the *Books in Canada* First Novel Award.

He has made two documentary films: *Sons of Captain Poetry*—on the work of poet bp Nichol, and *The Clinton Special*—about Theatre Passe Muraille's 'The Farm Show'. His stage version of *The Collected Works of Billy the Kid* has been performed in Canada and the U.S. as well as in Britain.